D1604922

Inside the Bees' Hive

by Karen Ang

Consultants:

Thomas D. Seeley, PhD
Department of Neurobiology and Behavior, Cornell University, Ithaca, New York

Kimberly Brenneman, PhD
National Institute for Early Education Research, Rutgers University, New Brunswick, New Jersey

BEARPORT
PUBLISHING

New York, New York

Credits

Cover, © irin-k/Shutterstock and © S & D & K Maslowski/FLPA; 3, 4 © iStockphoto/Thinkstock; 5, © S & D & K Maslowski/FLPA; 7, © Andre Skonieczny/Imagebroker/FLPA; 8, © Scott Camazine & Kirk Visscher/Getty Images; 9, © Lilkar/Shutterstock; 10, © Treat Davidson/FLPA; 11, © Konrad Wothe/Minden Pictures/FLPA; 12, © Dmitri Gomon/Shutterstock; 13, © Klagyivik Viktor/Shutterstock; 14, © Ted Kinsman/Science Photo Library; 15, © Imagebroker/FLPA; 16, 17TL, 17TR, © Wikipedia Creative Commons; 17B, © Horst Sollinger/Imagebroker; 18, © iStockphoto/Thinkstock; 19, © Tony Campbell/Shutterstock; 20, © S_E/Shutterstock; 21, © Darios/Shutterstock; 23TL, © StudioSmart/Shutterstock; 23TC, © S & D & K Maslowski/FLPA; 23TR, © Michael Avory/Shutterstock; 23BL, © Wikipedia Creative Commons; 23BC, © Treat Davidson/FLPA; 23BR, © Wikipedia Creative Commons.

Publisher: Kenn Goin
Senior Editor: Joyce Tavolacci
Creative Director: Spencer Brinker
Design: Emma Randall
Photo Researcher: Ruby Tuesday Books Ltd

Library of Congress Cataloging-in-Publication Data

Ang, Karen.
 Inside the bees' hive / by Karen Ang.
     p. cm. — (Snug as a bug: where bugs live)
 ISBN-13: 978-1-61772-905-8 (library binding)
 ISBN-10: 1-61772-905-1 (library binding)
 1. Bees—Behavior—Juvenile literature. 2. Beehives—Juvenile literature. I. Title.
 QL565.2.A54 2014
 595.79'9—dc23
                              2013004312

For more information, write to Bearport Publishing Company, Inc., 45 West 21st Street, Suite 3B, New York, New York 10010. Printed in the United States of America.

10 9 8 7 6 5 4 3 2 1

Contents

Welcome to the Hive

The sun is shining brightly in a forest.

A buzzing sound can be heard near some trees.

Suddenly, a small black-and-brown **insect** flies out of a hole high up in a tree.

It's a honey bee that has left its **hive** in search of food.

honey bee

honey bee

a honey bee hive inside a tree trunk

Honey bees make their homes inside hollow trees or on tree branches.

What Is a Bee?

A bee is a type of flying insect.

It has six legs, four wings, and two pointy antennae.

It collects all of its food from flowers.

There are about 20,000 kinds of bees in the world.

The small, fuzzy insect lives with thousands of other bees in a hive.

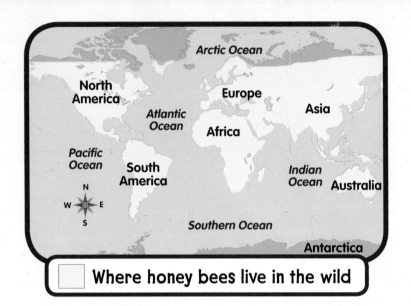

Where honey bees live in the wild

Bees live almost everywhere in the world. However, they do not live in very cold areas, such as Antarctica.

wings

antennae

legs

Building a Home

Inside a hive are combs made from **beeswax**.

Each comb is made up of many small rooms called cells.

To build a comb, bees make wax inside their bodies.

They then chew and press the wax to shape it into six-sided cells.

Honey bees join together hundreds of cells to form a comb.

beeswax

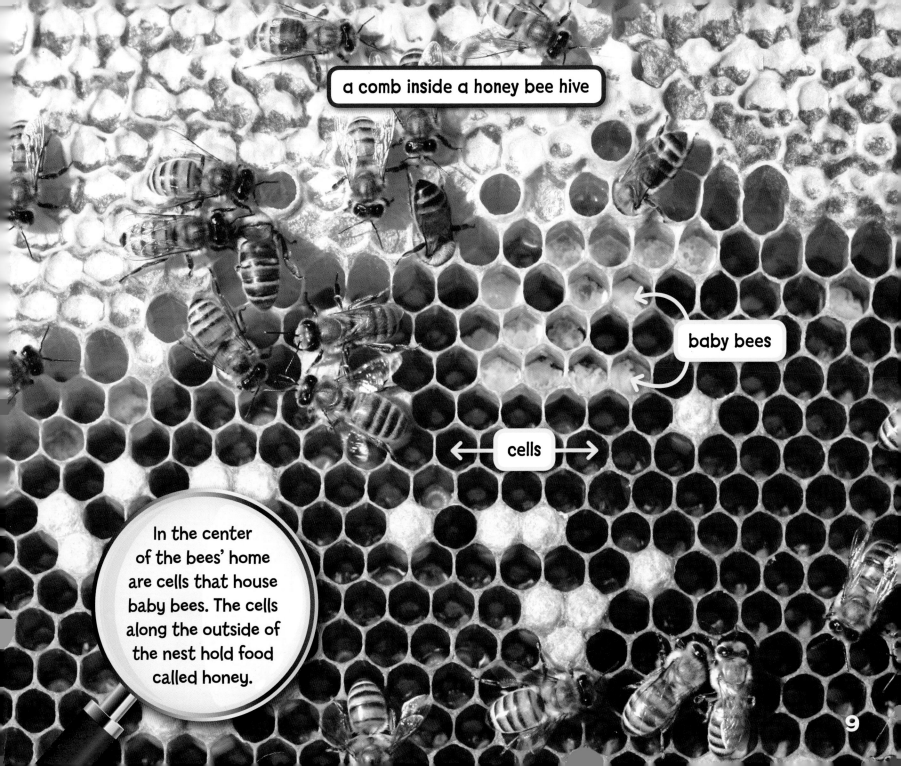

a comb inside a honey bee hive

baby bees

cells

In the center of the bees' home are cells that house baby bees. The cells along the outside of the nest hold food called honey.

A Bee Colony

A family of bees that live together in a hive is called a colony.

There are three types of bees in a colony.

The mother bee, or queen, lays eggs inside the hive.

Her sons, called drones, leave the hive to **mate** with other queens.

The queen's daughters are called worker bees.

They build combs, care for the young, and find food.

queen

drone

worker

Busy Bees

To find food, a worker bee searches for flowers.

The flowers are filled with a sugary liquid called nectar.

The bee goes inside the flowers to drink the nectar.

Then the worker flies back to its hive.

The worker stores the nectar in a cell, where it turns into sweet, sticky honey!

bee sipping nectar

Besides bees, what other animals do you think like to eat honey?

Workers also collect from flowers a yellow powder called pollen. Workers mix the pollen with nectar to make food for baby bees.

pollen

13

Protecting the Hive

Bees aren't the only animals that love the sweet taste of honey.

Bears tear open hives to eat the gooey food inside.

Luckily, bees have a way to protect their honey—and their hive.

Worker bees have sharp stingers that they can stick into an enemy's skin.

A bee's stinger contains poison that is very painful.

a worker bee's stinger

Some animals, like skunks and wasps, attack and eat honey bees. Bees also use their stingers to fight off these enemies.

a bear sniffing for honey

How do you think honey bees start their lives?

From Egg to Adult

Bees begin their lives as tiny eggs.

The queen lays the eggs inside cells in the center of the hive.

After three days, the eggs hatch into wormlike **larvae**.

About a week later, the larvae change into **pupae**.

After two weeks, the pupae become adult bees!

eggs

A queen can lay more than 1,000 eggs per day during the summer!

larvae

pupa

a baby bee hatching from its cell

How do you think a new hive forms?

A New Colony

Most of the young bees in a colony are workers or drones.

However, one of them may be a new queen.

Once there is a new queen bee, the colony might split up.

Almost always, the new queen stays in the hive to lay eggs.

The old queen and most of the workers fly off to start a new colony.

queen

bees looking for a new place to start a colony

Worker bees live for about a month, while queens can live for up to five years.

How do you think bees provide enough honey for millions of people to eat?

19

Keeping Bees

Most of the honey people eat doesn't come from bees that live in the wild.

Instead, it's collected from honey bees living inside wooden boxes.

The bees were put in the boxes by people called beekeepers.

Over time, the little insects built combs and raised their young there.

They also made lots of sweet, delicious honey for people to enjoy!

beehives

Science Lab

Build Your Own Comb

Imagine you are a beekeeper who teaches people all about honey bees and their hives.

Create a comb that will help your friends and family understand what a beehive is like.

Read the questions below and think about the answers. You can include this information as you talk about your honeycomb with friends and family.

What's inside a beehive?

What do the different bees do inside the hive?

Why is a hive a good place for bees to live?

How to make a comb

You will need:
- Scissors
- An empty cardboard paper towel tube
- Glue
- A rubber band
- Colored pencils and paper

1. Have an adult help you cut the paper towel tube into seven shorter tubes.

2. Place glue on the outside of the short tubes and stick them together, creating a pattern like a honey bee's comb. Put a large rubber band around the connected tubes to hold them together.

3. Using the colored paper and pencils, draw the three different types of bees that live in a colony. Then cut them out, and place them in and around the comb.

Science Words

beeswax (BEEZ-*waks*) a yellow substance that is made by bees and used to build their combs

hive (HIVE) a container housing the thousands of bees in a honey bee colony

insect (IN-sekt) a small animal that has six legs, three main body parts, two antennae, and a hard outer covering

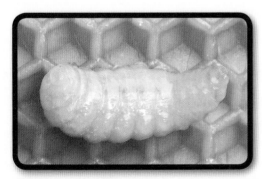

larvae (LAR-vay) young insects that have hatched from eggs but do not yet look like adults

mate (MAYT) the act of a male and a female coming together to have young

pupae (PYOO-pee) young insects at the stage of development between larvae and adults

Index

Read More

Lawrence, Ellen. *What Lily Gets from Bee (Plant-ology).* New York: Bearport (2013).

Winchester, Elizabeth. *Bees! (TIME for Kids Science Scoops).* New York: HarperCollins (2005).

Learn More Online

To learn more about bees and their hives, visit **www.bearportpublishing.com/SnugasaBug**

About the Author

Karen Ang has worked on many books about science, nature, and animals. She lives in Connecticut, where she loves to watch the honey bees fly from flower to flower.